Covid-19 A Sketchbook:
Letters to Daddy

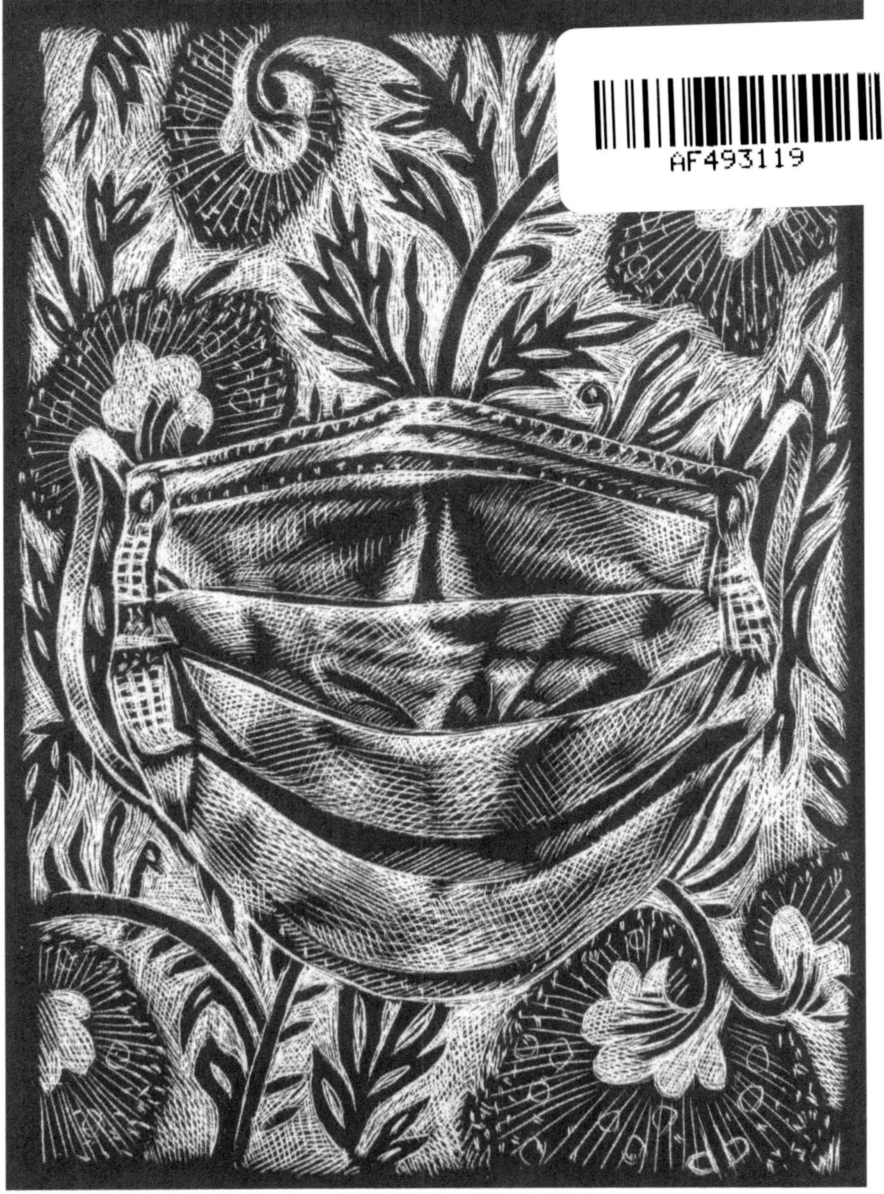

Written and Illustrated by CD Bolinger

DEDICATION

This Sketchbook is dedicated to the loving memory of my parents, Gary and Carolyn Bolinger and to all The Helpers.

February 14, 2020
Happy Valentine's Day Daddy-
  I used to bring Momma the white rose like
you always gave her for Valentine's Day but I
couldn't tell if she noticed & I stopped. I got
her a teddy bear once. She smiled at that.
There is a virus going around in Europe. It's
all over the news. I'll keep ya posted, I'm sure
it will be fine. It just feels off. Like how the air
used to smell like peaches out on the land
before a tornado. Other than that- everything
is fine. Jack is doing well at the Community
College and I'm still teaching the kiddos at the
High School. The ones that aren't glued to
their phones at least. My water heater broke
but I got it fixed. I swear with this old house
it's always something. Okay,
I miss you. Tell Mom Hi-Love-LDA

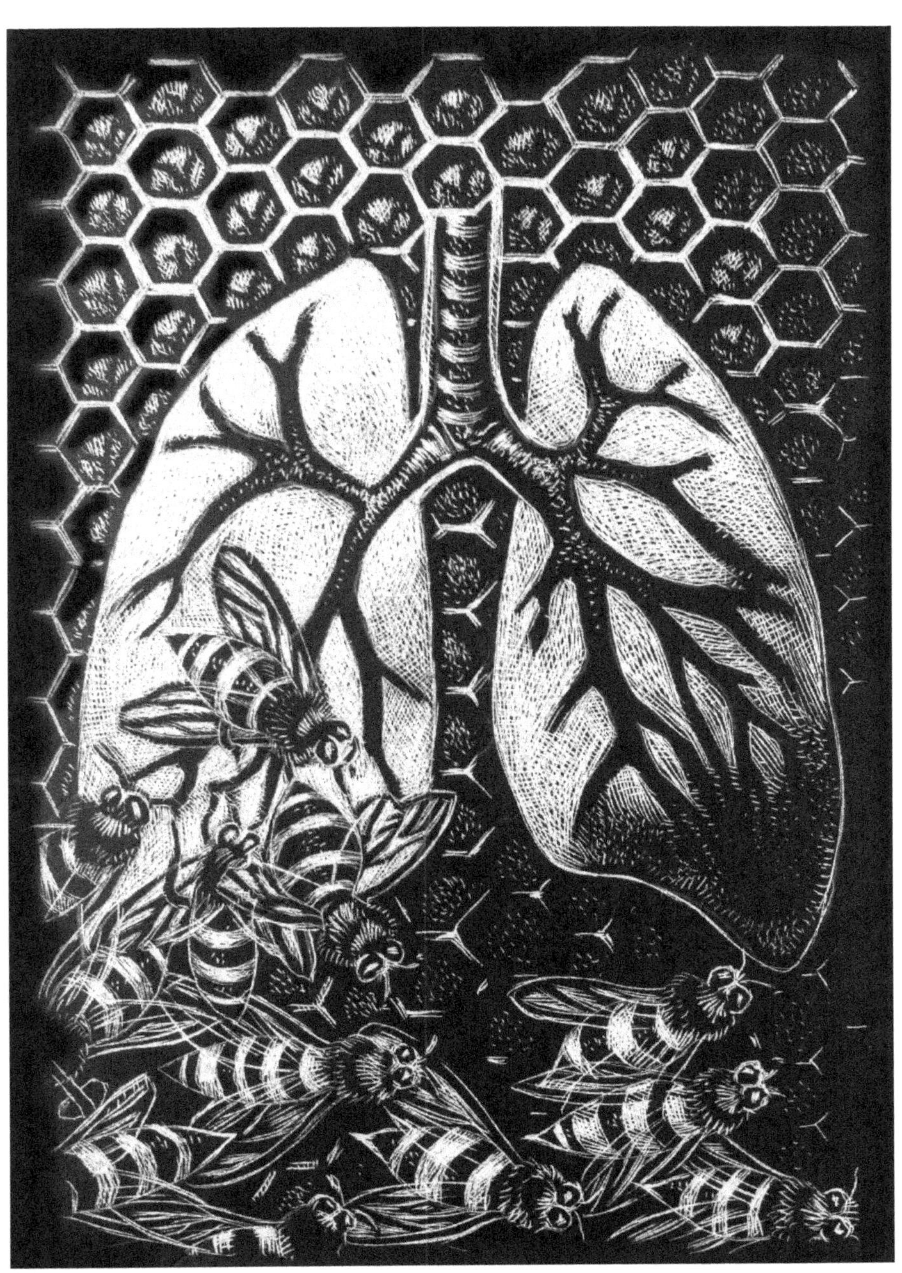

March 7, 2020
Hey Daddy,

So I went to the store today and probably bought more canned food and stuff than I needed. The store was fine but next week is Spring Break so I know the store will be packed. I hear your beloved Costco has been very busy. Did you know it took me years to finally finish off all those rolls of plastic bags you had? I saved the last one. I cried when I got down to the last one and then I laughed so hard that I was crying over a trash bag. I miss you -LDA

Late March
Hey Daddy- the shoppers have gone bat shit crazy now. Apparently they all want toilet paper? What the heck? I mean you can't find toilet paper anywhere. We are fine. Thanks to that prepper phase I went through years ago, we are fine on food. Maybe not on toilet paper. Then there are these jerks buying everything up. I gave Mrs. Cunning my flour and yeast in exchange for her fixing the bad binding I did on a quilt. Tell Mommy Hi. We love you-LDA

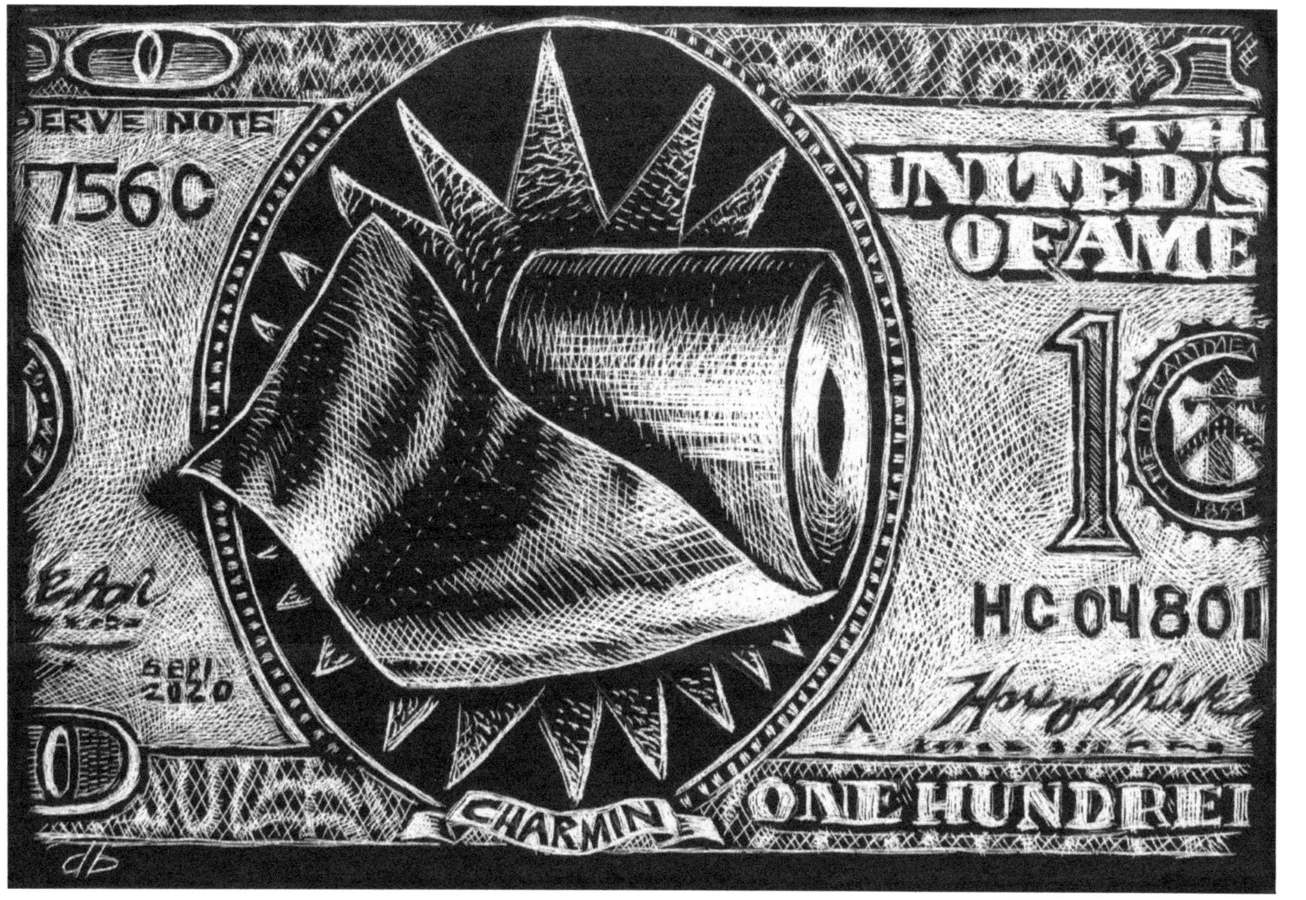

ERVE NOTE
756C
THI
UNITED S
OF AME
1C
HC 04801
SEPT 2020
CHARMIN
ONE HUNDREI

March 28, 2020
Hey Daddy,
I never got to tell you & Mommy what happened when I went to get some fabric cut months ago. I asked the lady cutting my fabric where she was from and she said Poolville. I said we used to live there. She says "OH! Did you know Mrs. Bolinger? She was the best teacher ever! My son had her for Pre-K!" I told her "Yes, my son had her too, she was great". I made it to the parking lot before I started crying. Mommy really was the best teacher ever. Love ya both- talk later- LDA.

April 6,
Hey Daddy,
Teaching online sucks. I have no idea how many of my kids have access to computers or if they have to share with siblings or parents or both. Maybe they have to work? Maybe their parents got laid off and they are hungry? I worry about them. Some of my students have been turning in small stuff online. The Seniors are really bummed about Prom. Love ya- LDA

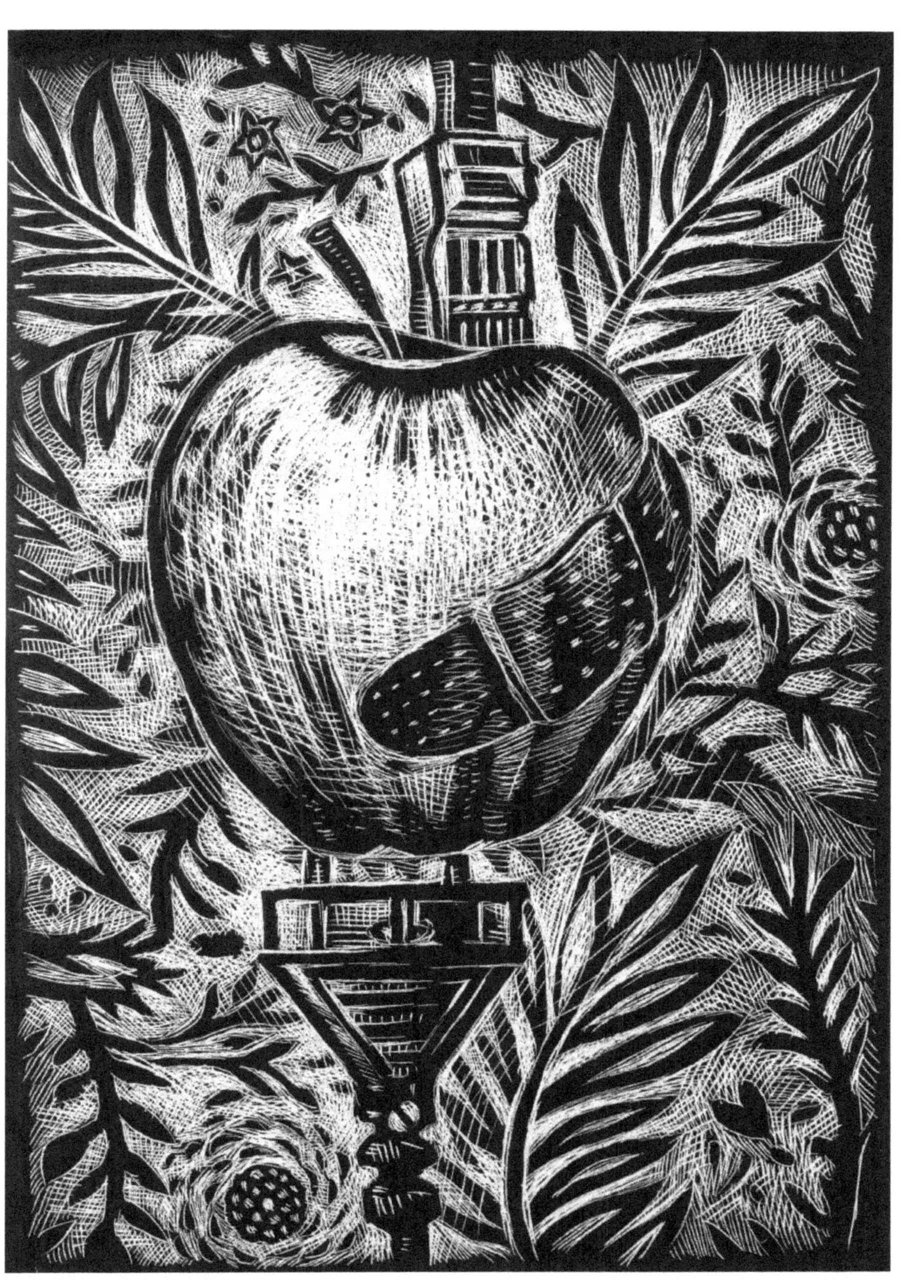

April 2020,

I can't imagine what you thought when I moved to New York after College to "become an ARTIST!" Thanks for not telling me. It was a wonderful time & I loved it. It really is a Wonder City. Thanks for talking me out of trying to walk out of it with a 5 month old Jack when 9-11 hit. Thanks for being a calm voice on the other end of the phone. I still can't watch anything about that day. I refuse to.

New York is getting hit hard by the Pandemic but Governor Cuomo is amazing! He reminds me of you. He is calm and tells me the facts but he is also reassuring. I like watching his reports. I do not like watching Trump. Everyone is in Quarantine. For me and Jack, it's okay. We are mild hermits anyway and lucky enough that I have a job. I can't imagine being in New York in some of those small apartments and not being able to leave. I took Jack there for 11 days as his present from graduating High School. He loved seeing where he was from. I loved showing him our old neighborhood and meeting old friends. I worry about them now. I love you. I miss you. Tell Mom hi-LDA

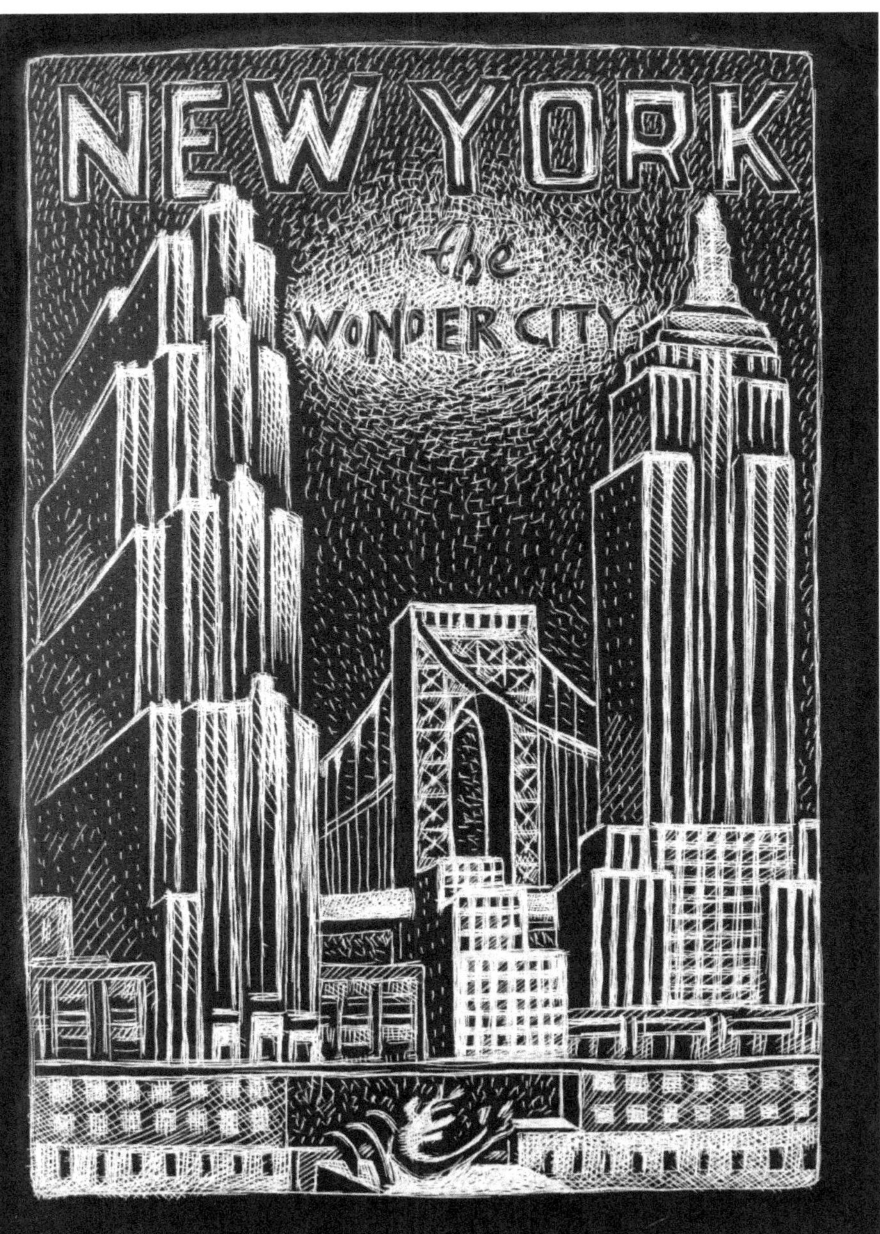

NEW YORK
the
WONDER CITY

May 2020,

Hey Daddy,

I remember watching Mr. Rogers on TV as a child. I remember that he told us kiddos to "Look for the helpers". There are a lot of Helpers now. They call them "Essential". I tried to draw them as playing cards, they are all Kings and Queens.

The Doctors and Nurses on the frontlines are risking their lives all over the world to help. They don't even have the equipment to keep themselves safe.

The Grocery workers going to work with mobs of the panic filled public in their face.

The City workers like our trash pick-up, utility, truck drivers, all those things that keep our lives running that we take for granted.

The Police and Fire Departments that continue to answer calls and put out fires and are too often the first responders in an emergency.

For all the bad that humans can do to each other, there are always the good people, the helpers to even it out. Thanks for letting me watch Mr. Rogers. Love you. Tell Mommy hi.- LDA.

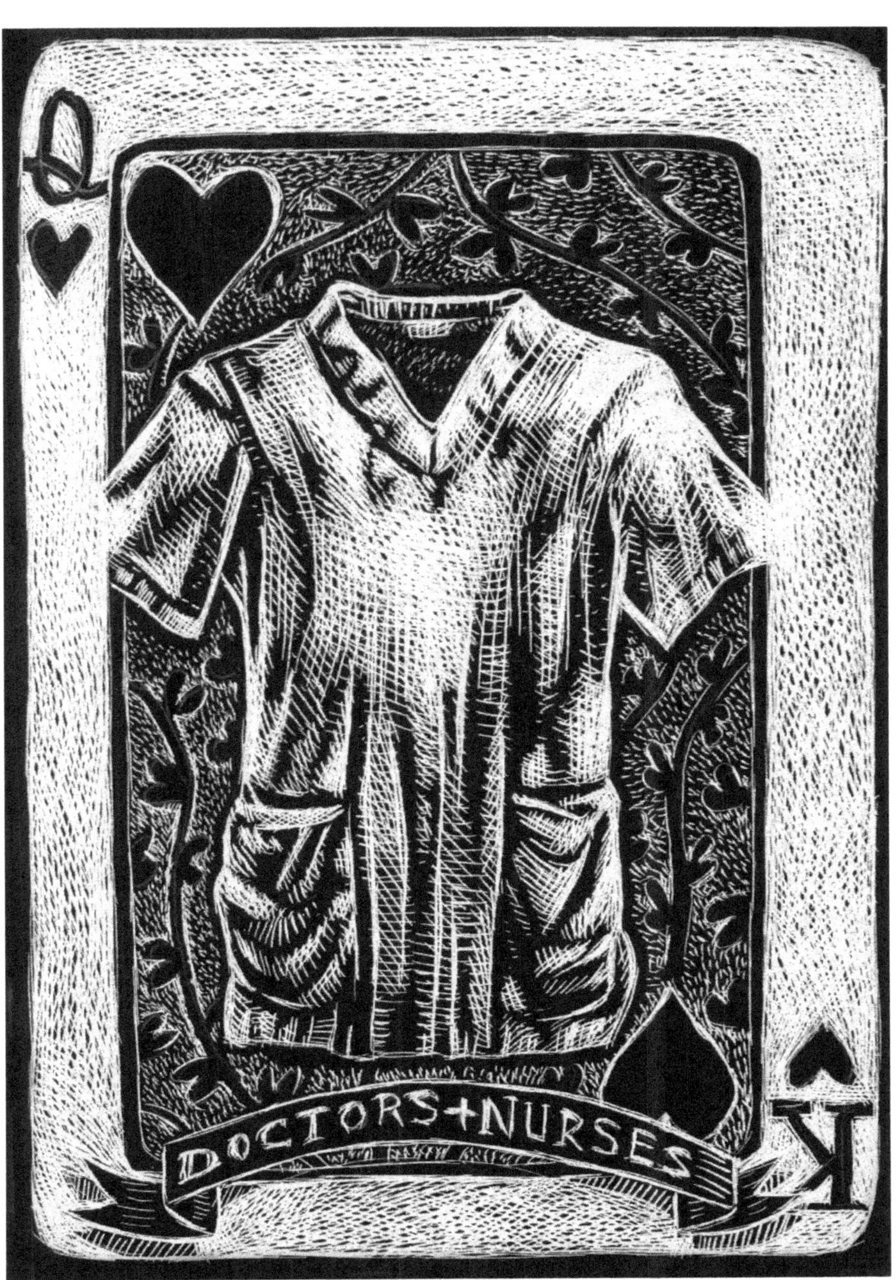

Q
DOCTORS+NURSES
K

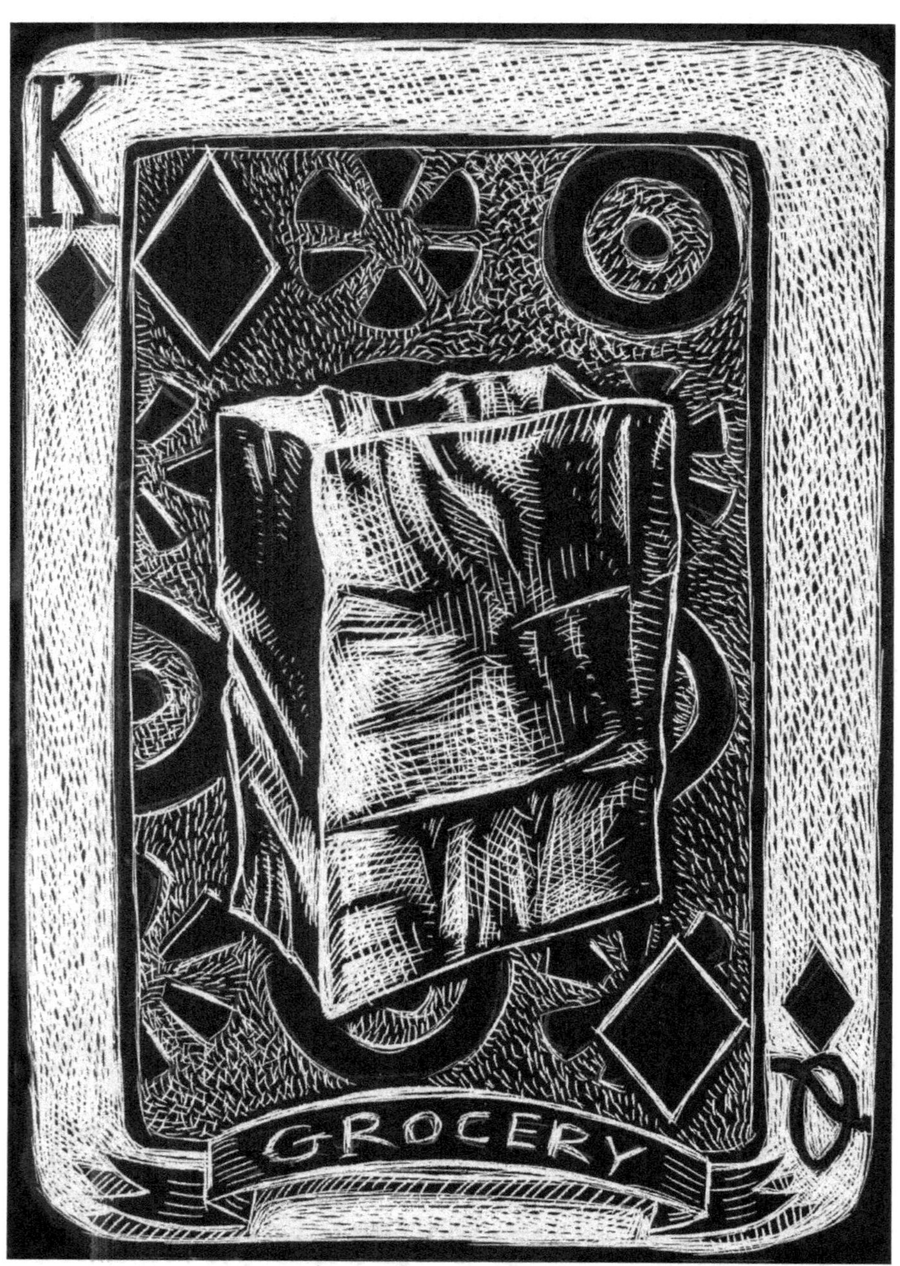

K
GROCERY

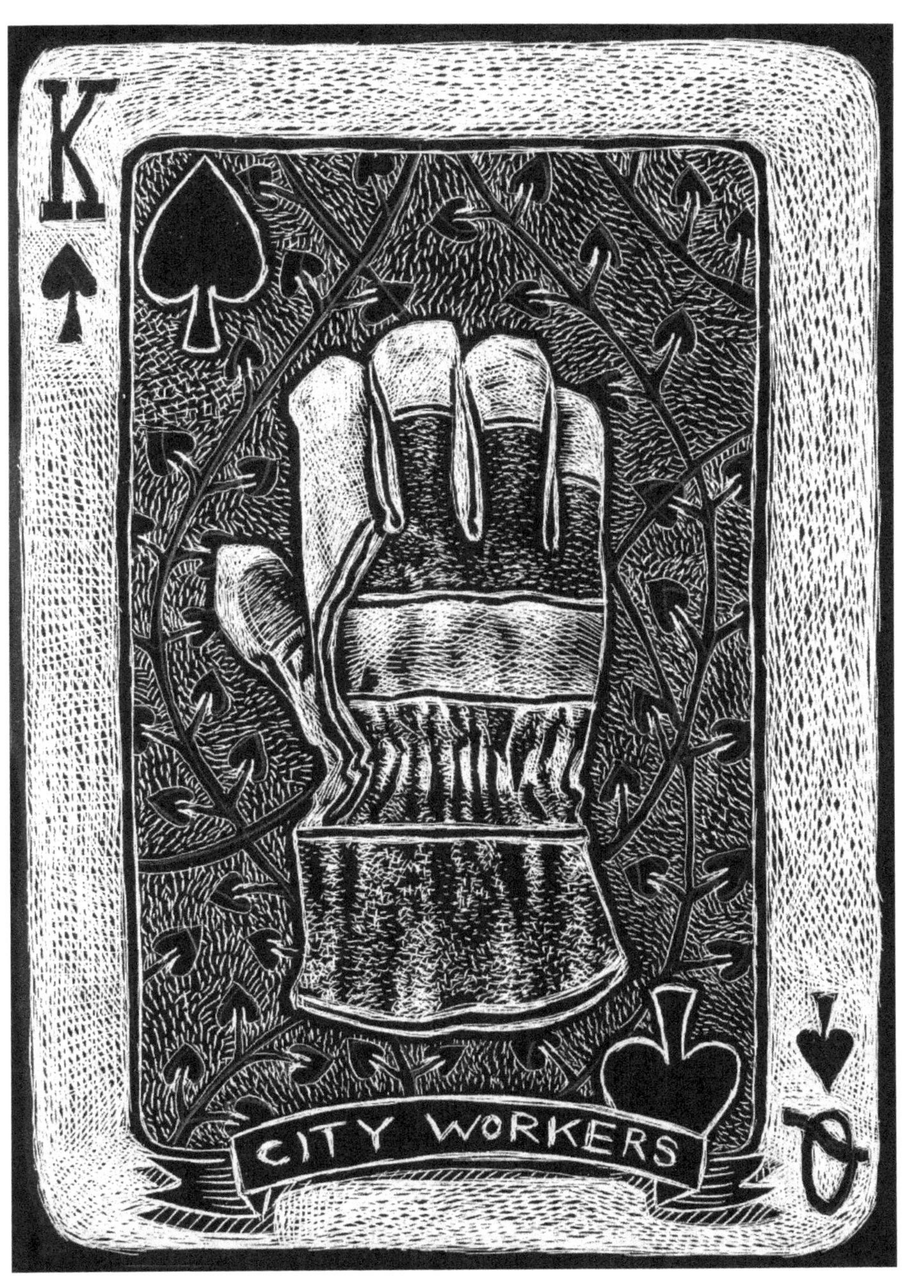
K
CITY WORKERS

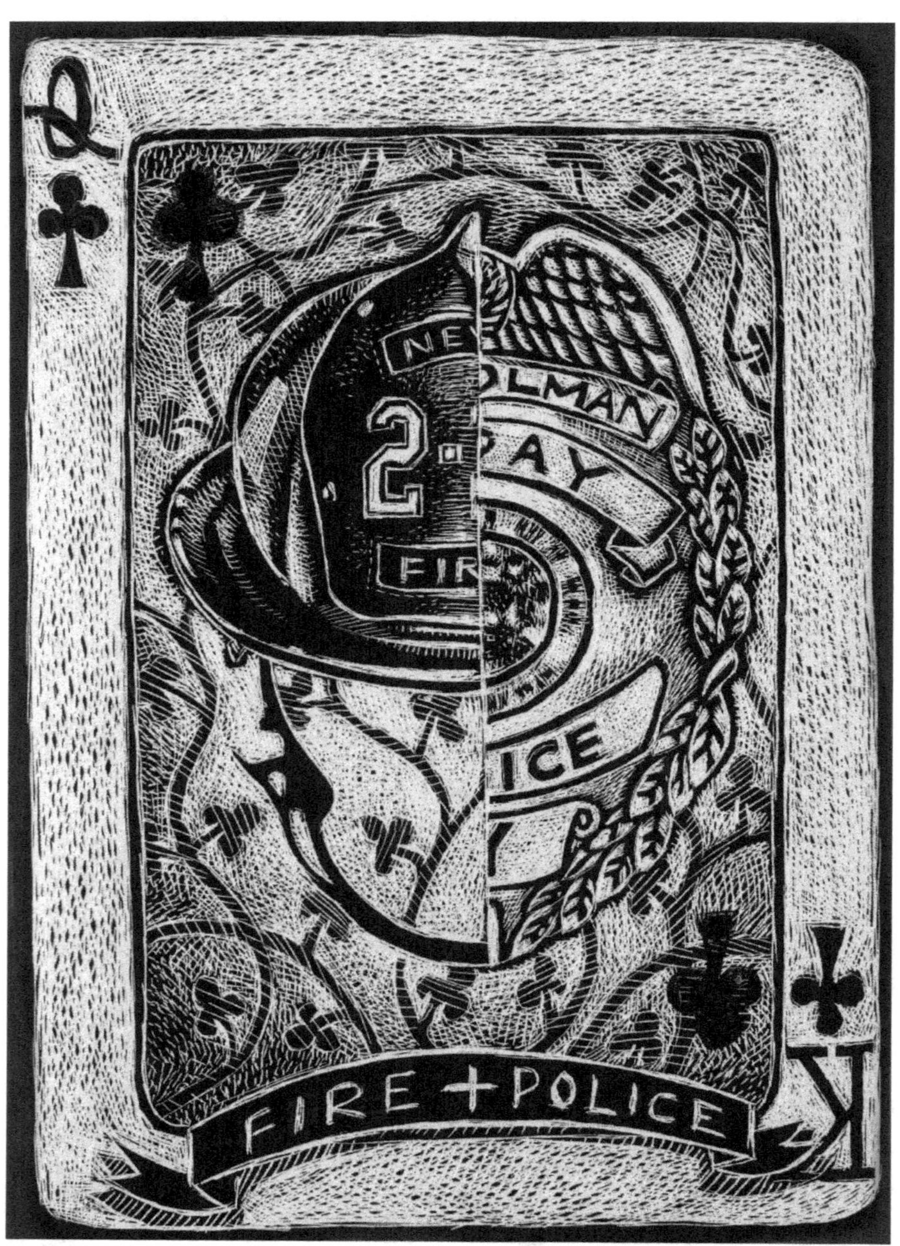
Q
NE
OLMAN
2
PAY
FIR
ICE
FIRE + POLICE
K

May 2020
Hey Daddy,

So you've missed a bit of Jack growing up. I'm so glad we got to live with you guys when we came back from New York for a bit. Those were good years and thanks for taking us in. I wish you and momma could see him now.

He has this big beard and its red! His father passed soon after you and we went to Minnesota for the funeral. We are still close with his family and his older sisters. He went to Ireland all on his own for a few months and stayed in hostels and navigated the buses and all the other surprises that come with a trip overseas very well. I was a nervous wreck but he came back safe and certainly has the travel bug now. He is brilliant when it comes to History and seems to have memorized all important dates. He loves to debate history and politics with me and he has a wicked sense of humor. I think you would like the young man he has become. We are spending a lot of time together like most families now and although he works out every day- he still eats top ramen when he gets too lazy to cook. I love you Guys- Please watch out for my Boy-LDA.

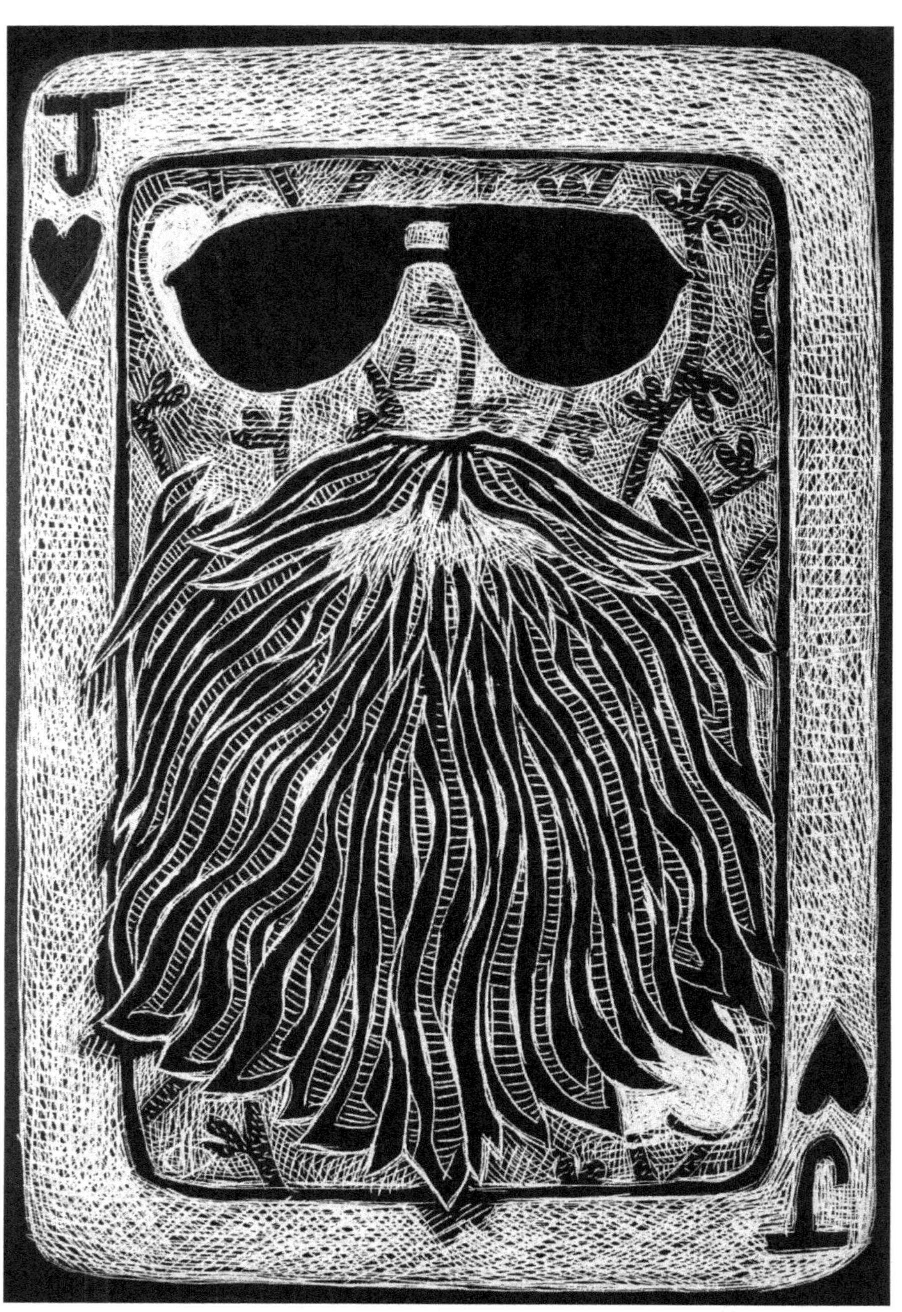

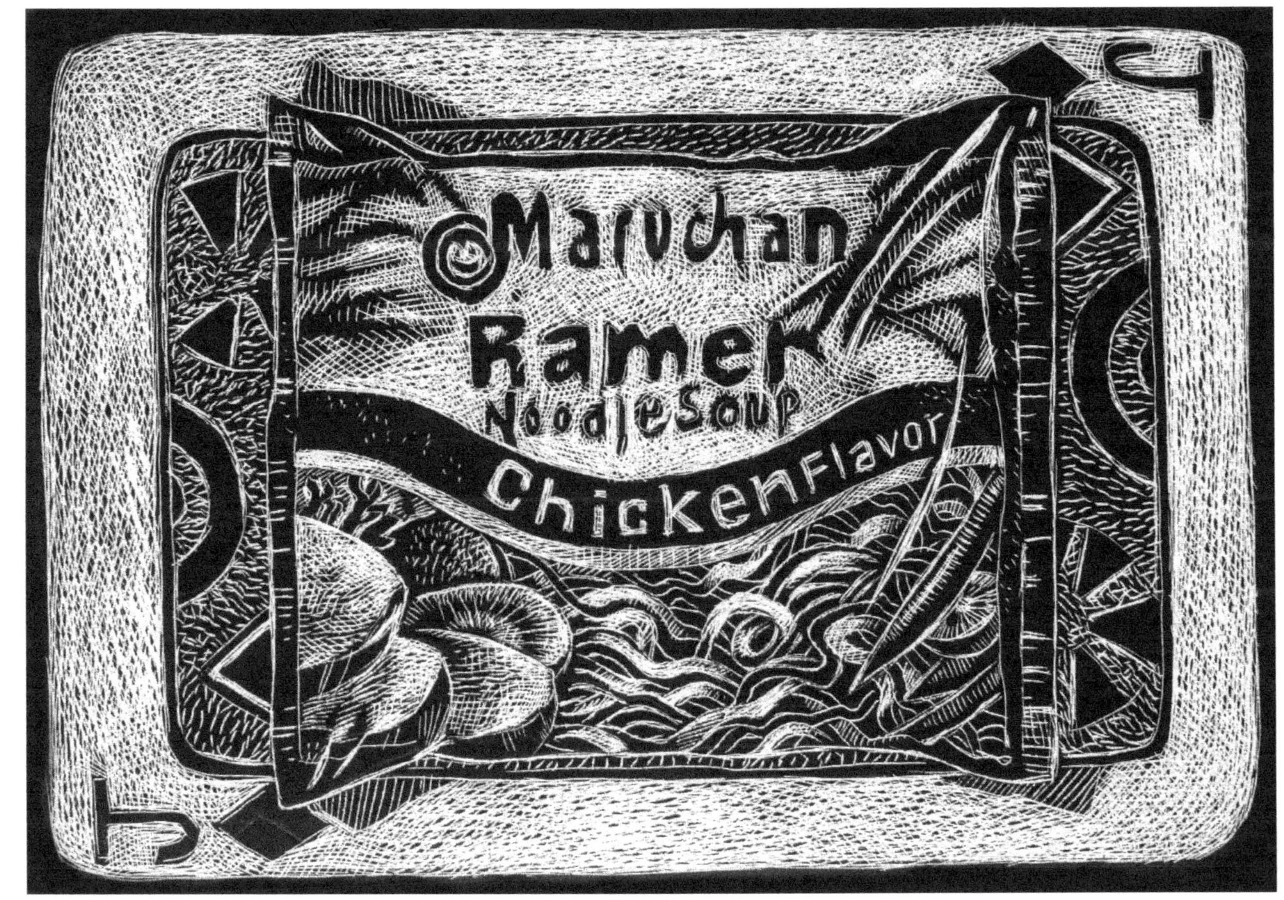

J
Maruchan
Ramen
Noodle Soup
Chicken Flavor
J

May 2020,
Hey Daddy,

So Jack and I have a new weird ritual. Every night at 7pm we sit down and watch an episode of Star trek Next Generation. We were watching one episode one night when Jack started going "I remember this! I was sitting on the big black couch next to Grampa eating goldfish!" It was the episode where Wesley broke something in the Eden Society and he was going to be killed. We are not very fond of the Wesley episodes but I love our little 7pm ritual.

I really like that I like my son as a person. I enjoy spending time with him. People say I'm a good mom but really I just try to be half as good as you and Momma were. You really were kind, funny people and Kathy and I got lucky to have you.

Jack and I finished Next Generation and have now moved on to Deep Space Nine. It's not as good but some episodes are great. I mainly just watch it to keep our ritual going. I love you and I love Mamma- Tell her hi for me- LDA.

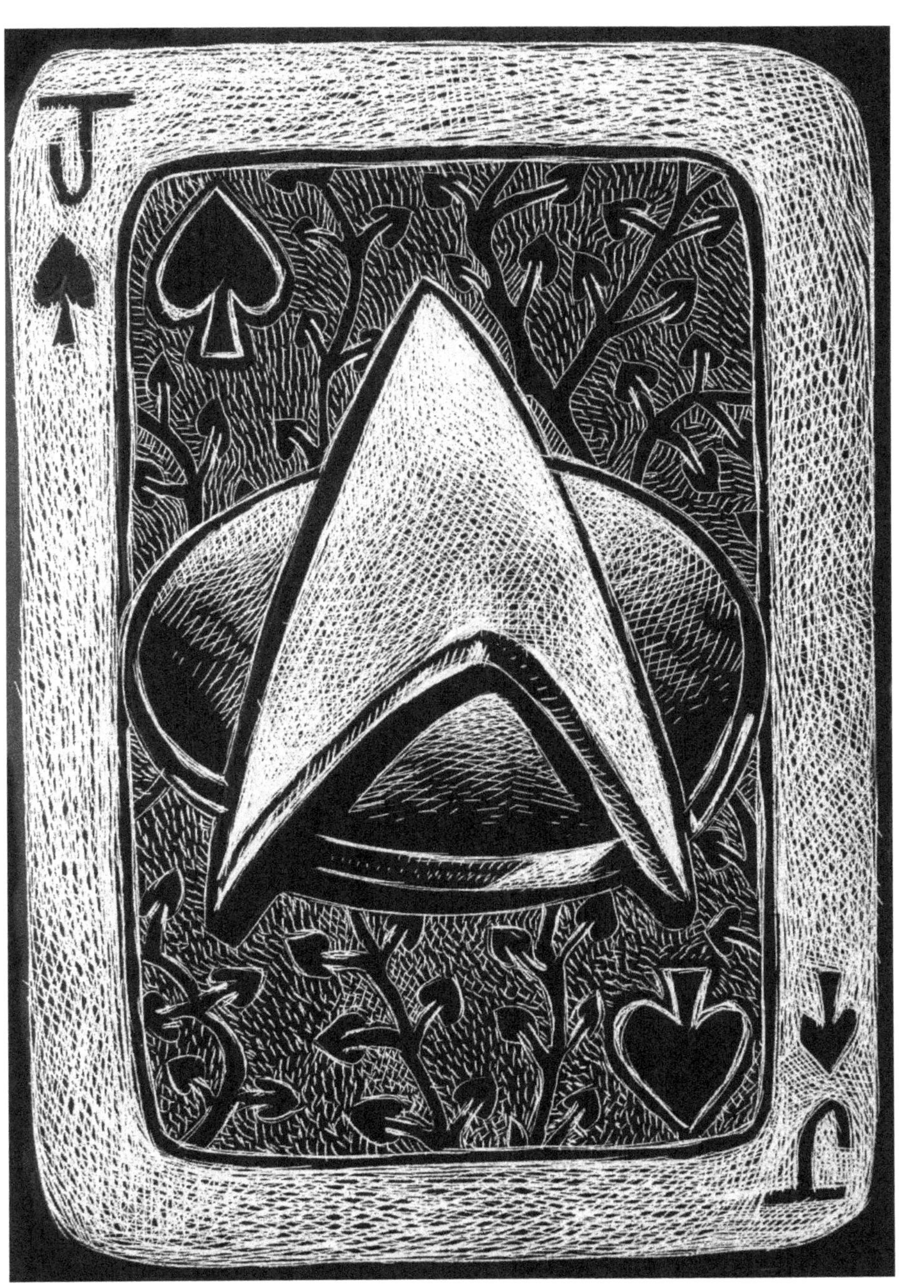

May 2020
Hey Daddy,
   I don't know where to begin about Trump.
Do you remember my 4th Grade Teacher Mrs.
Goodwin? She was so kind to me & she always
said "If you can't say something nice, don't say
anything at all." So…

Love ya- tell Mom Hi-LDA

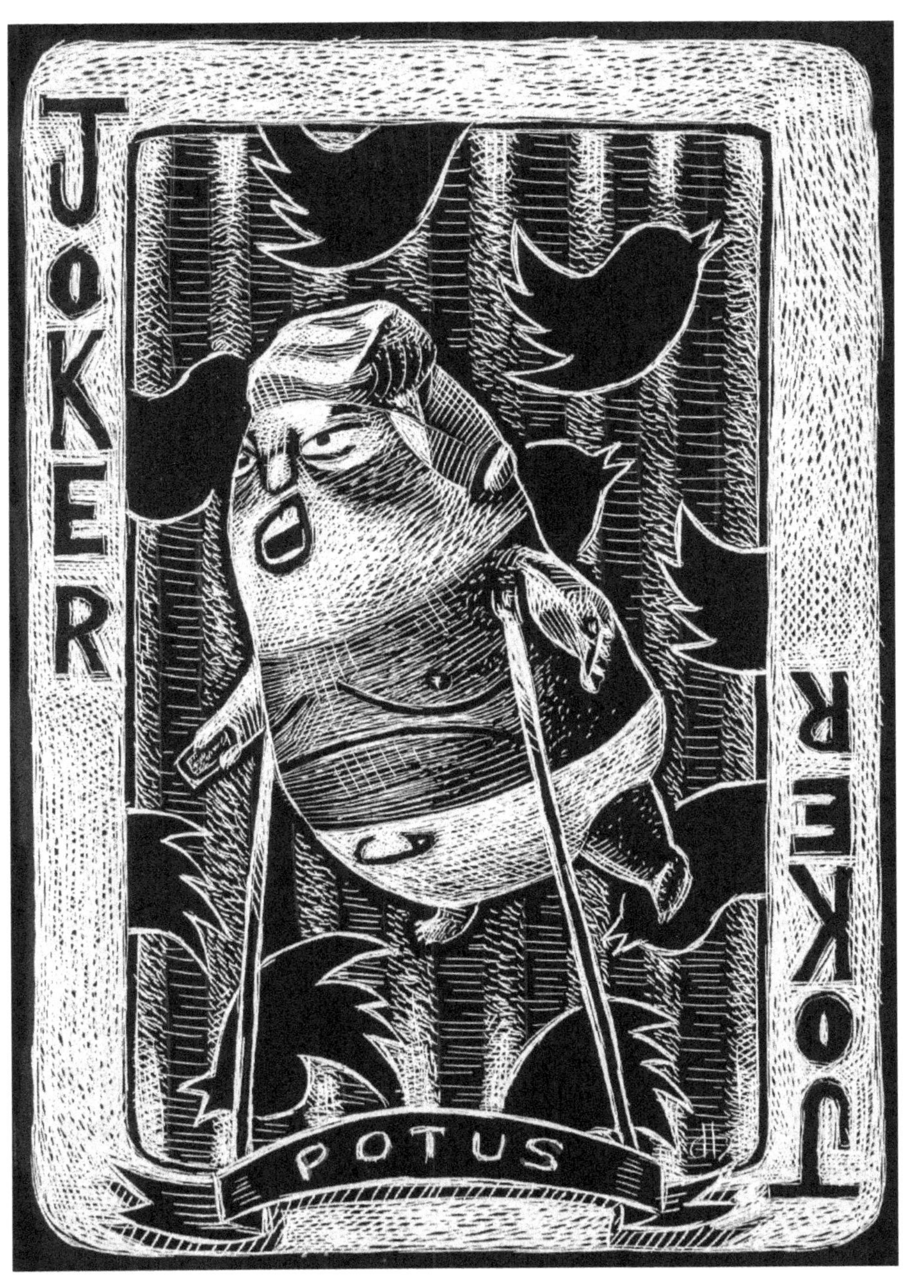
JOKER
JOKER
POTUS

May 2020,
Hey Daddy,

I know you never planned on having two daughters but you did a great job. You taught me to shoot a bb gun and tried to teach me to drive stick but we both know that didn't end well. You didn't laugh at me when I got that awful haircut my senior year. You carried me when I had chicken pox so bad I couldn't walk and you drove us to the hospital when Jack broke his arm. I never understood how much you loved us until I had Jack. A close friend of mine has been trying to get pregnant and finally did. Sadly she miscarried. At the same time I had a former student of mine texting me during her delivery! How cool is that? I mean, I know we get attached to some of our students but that struck me as such a sweet thing. After a hard delivery Madeline Grace has entered the world.

With the Pandemic and the Quarantine and so much uncertainty about the future…It is a testimony to the human race that we just keep going. That babies will be born and loved even in the strangest of times. Thanks for being My Daddy-Love you & Momma- LDA

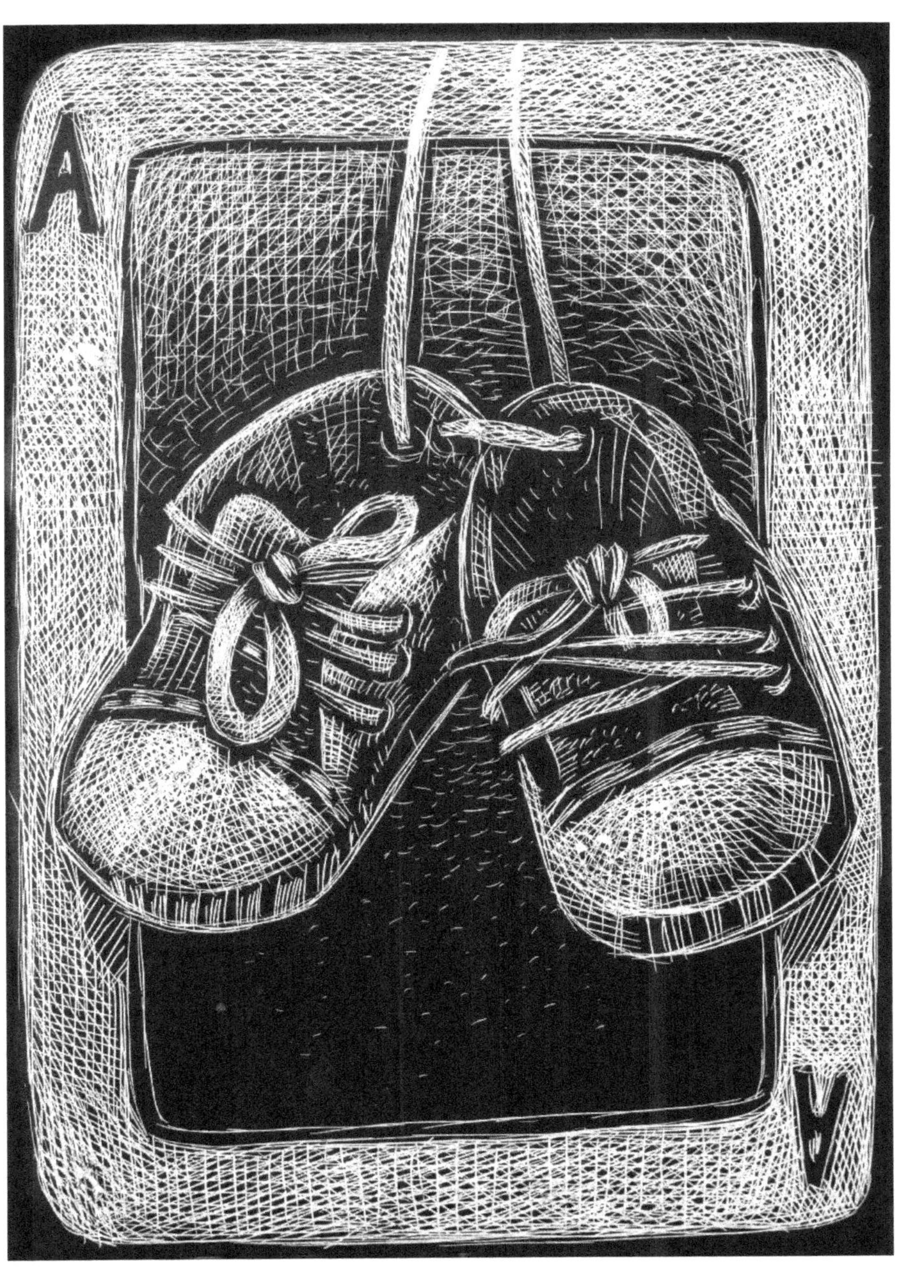

May 2020,
Hey Daddy,

Many States are starting to open up a wee bit. I finally got those masks I ordered in February and I wear mine. Some people don't. We are close to 100,000 people dead in the USA and over a million dead worldwide.

My friend Sally went grocery shopping and was wearing a mask. A total stranger said "OH, You're one of those sheep that believes this shit!." Sally was stunned. She's just trying to get some veggies for dinner. I got dirty looks at Brookshire's but at Albertsons it's okay. So now I only go to Albertsons. Were people always so mean? Wearing a mask simply implied I believe the science and am trying to keep people safe. But so many people take it as a political statement and everything political now is crazy.

I was trying to turn onto my street and there was a car in front of me. He had plenty of time to turn & started to turn but an oncoming car sped up on purpose. The car in front of me slowed down to a crawl just to be spiteful as well. I told you, people are just being mean.
Miss You, Love You-LDA

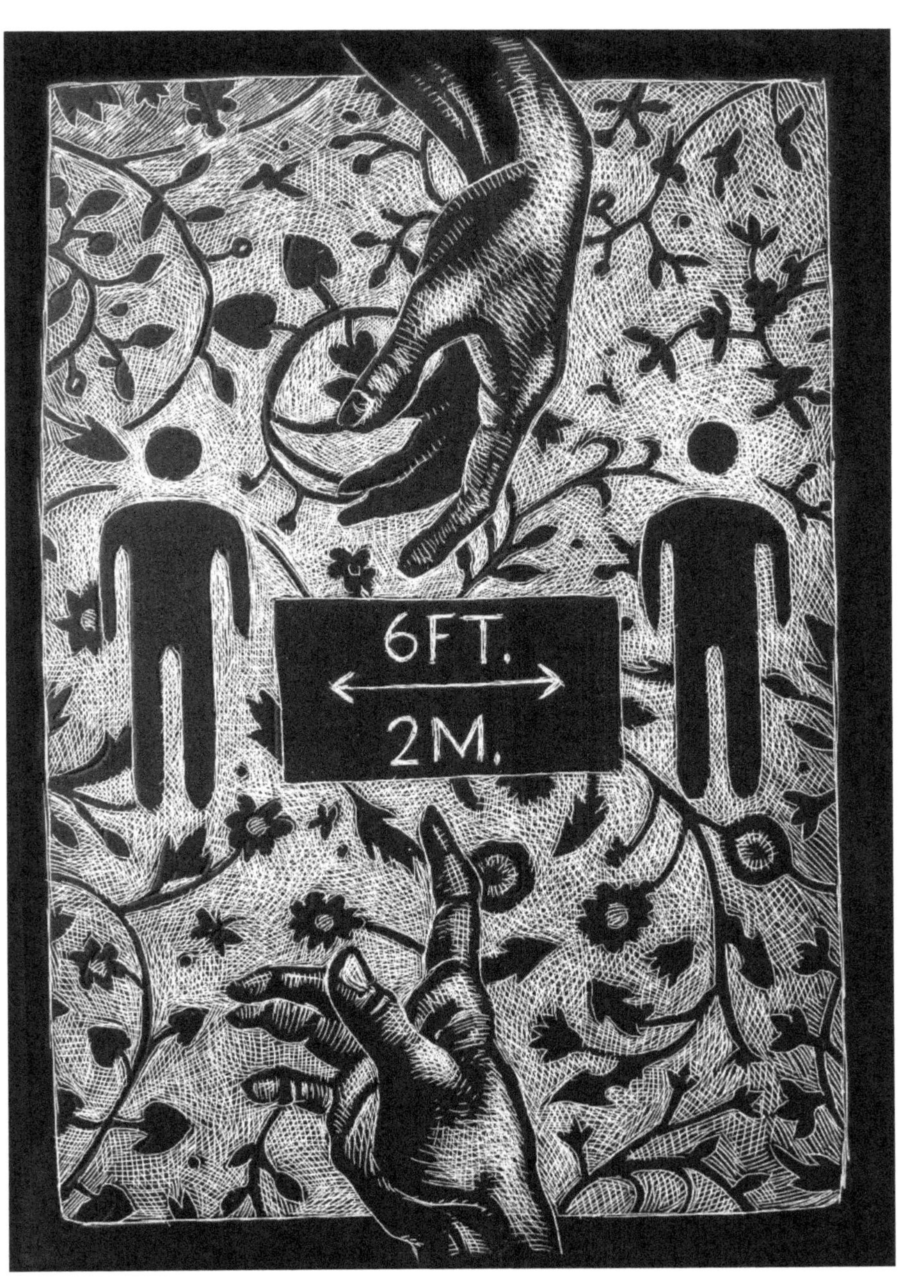

6FT.
2M.

May 2020,

Hey Daddy,

I know I've never had Mom's Green thumb but I try. The weather has been absolutely beautiful in the 70's and just enough rain to keep everything green. I've been working in the back yard a lot. It takes my mind off of the news.

They say that India's air quality is the best it's been in ages. Without all the cars and airplanes running all over the world the Earth seems to have gotten a break from us annoying humans. I think it is a good thing. The Earth needs so much help. I worry what it will be like when Jack has kids. I worry about the bees. I worry about the ocean and the air. I worry about the ice caps and the single use plastic filling the landfills. I worry about the forests that are getting stripped bare. I worry that we are at a tipping point and we won't be able to save it. Don't get me wrong, there are lots of people worried. At least for now, Momma earth can catch her breath a bit. I'm glad we got to grow up in nature on the land. Love you. Tell Mom Hi-LDA.

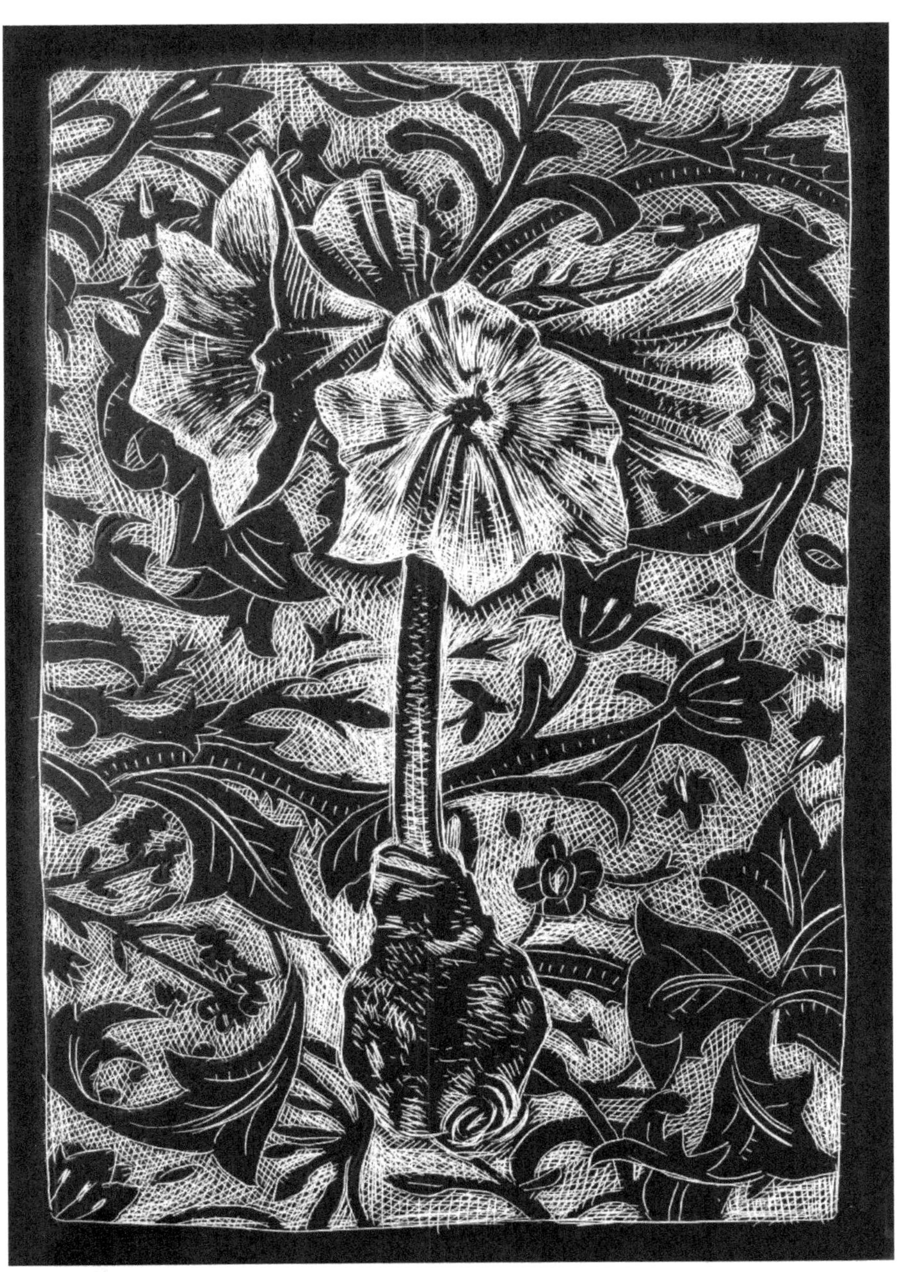

MARCH 25TH, 2020

Daddy,
  The world just watched a man die on TV. He couldn't breathe. He called for his Momma. I have no words.

June 10, 2020
Hey Daddy,
America has been protesting every night in almost every city. Some were rioting and looting and burning buildings but that has calmed down now. We watched on TV as peaceful protesters were teargassed and shot with rubber bullets because Trump wanted a photo op. They were peaceful!
  Things need to change. I really hope they do. All those sappy TV commercials keep saying how we are "All in this Together" but I don't think I have ever seen America so divided in my lifetime. I love you Daddy, tell Mom Hi-
LDA

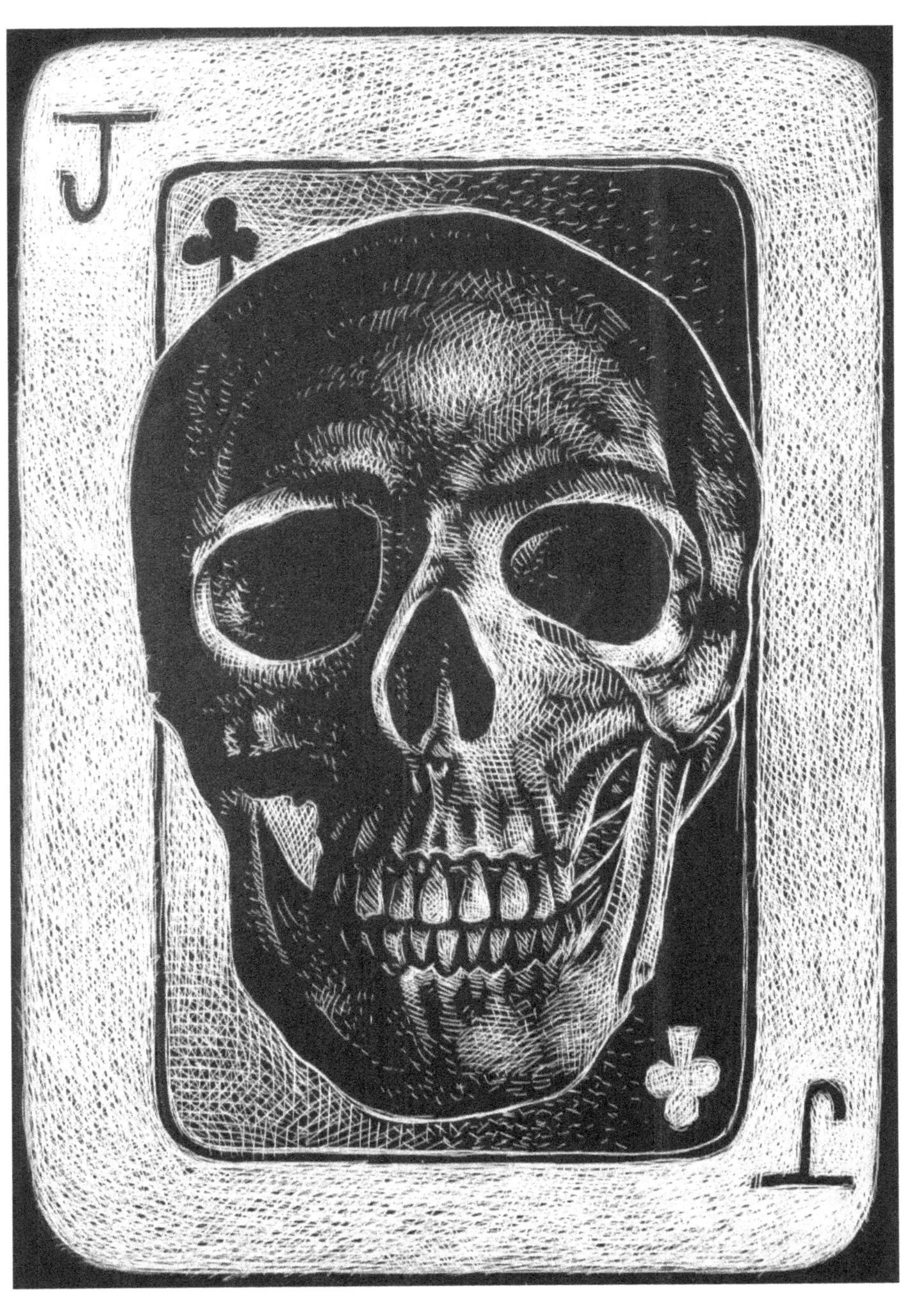

J
♣
J
♣

June 5, 2020

Dear Reader,
  This sketchbook began as my first attempt at The Brooklyn Sketchbook Project. I had no idea when it started how things would unfold in the world.
  My father passed years ago from Diabetes and my mother passed soon after from Parkinson's. I was honored to be with her when she passed and miss them both very much.
  I hope the world finds a better was to embrace The Golden Rule. Treat others as you would like to be treated.
  The artwork included in my sketchbook was created by sgraffito. Sgraffito is a method of scratching through a surface to reveal a lower layer of a contrasting color . Thank you for taking the journey with me.

Sincerely,
 CD. Bolinger
 (LDA)

Daddy & Me-mid 80s

I don't remember exactly where this was taken
but I do remember Momma made the dress I
was wearing and Daddy smelled like Brut
cologne and pipe smoke. Like always.

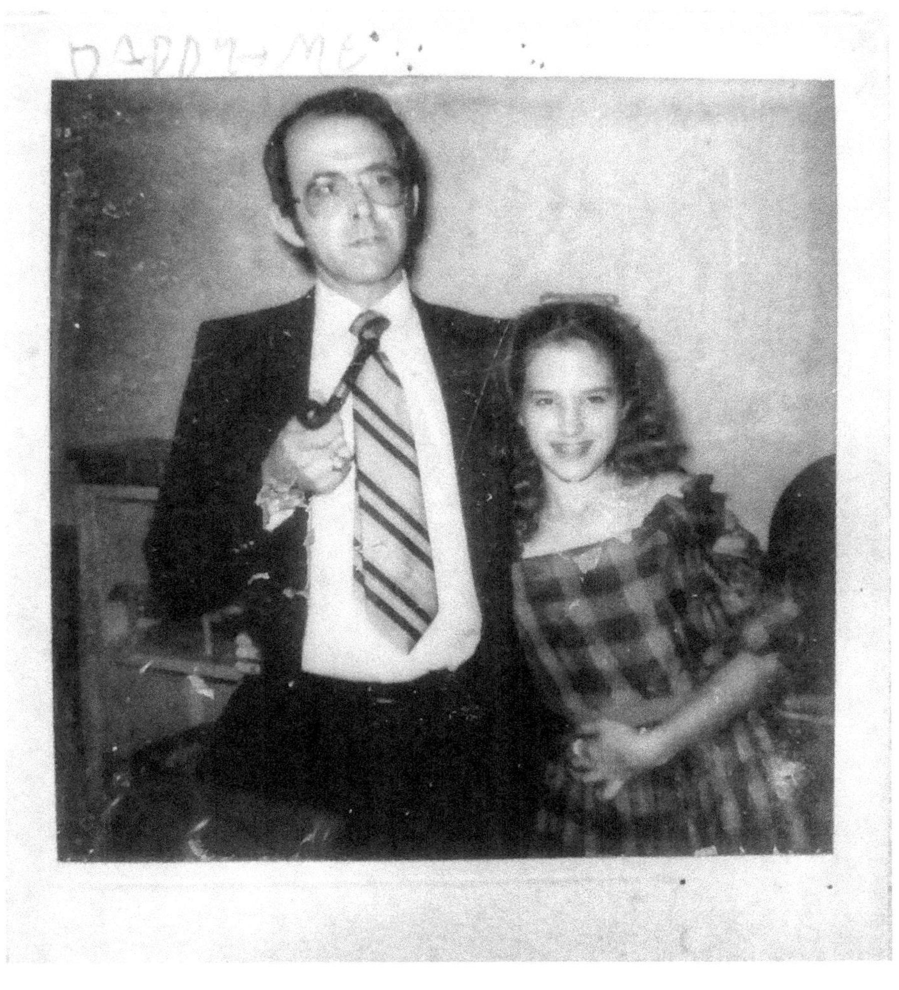

www.ingramcontent.com/pod-product-compliance
Lightning Source LLC
Chambersburg PA
CBHW070327160726
47999CB00003B/1192